Breathing Room

Breathing Room

POEMS OF REST & RETREAT

James Crews

MANDALA

SAN RAFAEL LOS ANGELES LONDON

Sometimes the most important

thing in a whole day

is the rest we take

between two deep breaths.

—Etty Hillesum

CONTENTS

Introduction

The Practice of Rest

I was lying on the couch in the middle of the morning, half in and out of sleep. The day had barely begun, but already fatigue draped itself over me like a weighted blanket. Outside, spring had sprung, and the warmer sun we'd waited for all winter now slanted like a spill of honey across the floor. Normally, it would be beckoning me outside for a walk or work in the perennial gardens we tend each year, yet I could hardly lift myself into the shower. My daily cup of strong coffee had almost no effect, and I felt excited about nothing. Having spent the past several months traveling back and forth across the country, climbing on and off planes for work, it became clear: I was facing burnout.

For years now, I have had a daily practice of sitting at my desk with a notebook and pen, just letting the words carry me forward wherever they want to go. I am always surprised by what comes, thrilled if anything at all appears on the page. During this period, however, even the writing—one of my deepest joys—began to suffer. I'd find myself in the middle of composing a poem and would have to stop before I'd finished, with no energy to push ahead. This was when alarm bells really went off for me. I had always been able to fall back on my creativity during times of crisis and difficulty—when my father died twenty-five years ago, when my mother and both grandmothers died all within six months of each other, through job losses and the heartbreak of fractured friendships. My notebook has been with me through it all, able to contain my pain and guide me back toward presence and grace, like a faithful companion. This time, the well had run dry. Nothing seemed to relieve me of my constant fatigue and numbness toward life.

I wish I could say I found an instant cure that brought me back from the brink. But the answer is more complicated than that. After seeing my doctor to be sure that nothing else was physically wrong with me, and after seeing my therapist regularly again, I realized what I needed: more rest. I needed long stretches of quiet that bring with them a sense of relief and release from the self. As I battled each day with the voices in my head that said I wasn't doing enough, and was just being lazy, I saw that rest itself could become a practice, perhaps supported by writing, meditation, prayer, and whatever else helps us to enter a space beyond the noise and busyness of our lives, even if just for a few minutes at a time. It dawned on me that any form of rest we decide to offer ourselves can become a necessary and sacred pause.

I remember watching my husband dig in the rocky Vermont earth around our house, planting trees, shrubs, and flowers for the pollinators and birds in our corner of the woods. Digging here is no easy thing. Every time the shovel reaches into the ground, you'll hear the telltale clink that means you have struck some buried stone. That morning, I stood at the window as Brad lifted rock after rock out of the earth and stacked them in a small pile beside holes that would soon house viburnum, black-eyed Susans, echinacea, and Japanese anemones, which send out the smallest, most delicate pink flowers at the end of summer. It occurred to me that I needed to do some digging myself and gently remove whatever was blocking me from feeling fully alive, from being here. I needed to make space in the ground of myself for what needed to grow, spread, stretch out. And I knew it would take months of what Buddhists often call "effortless effort," the practice of doing less yet somehow accomplishing more. This meant letting go of my unrealistic schedule, and becoming less "productive" in the outward sense of the word, focusing instead on what genuinely called to me.

Because our culture teaches us that striving and pushing are the only ways to achieve success and make a living, we begin to believe it. What if we measured true success not by our bank accounts or professional achievements, not by number of followers or material possessions, but instead by how rested we feel each day, how awake we are to ourselves and our loved ones? The poems you hold in your hand are the direct result of living this question every day and every moment that I could for the past several years. I honestly wasn't sure if these poems would ever be published, and I certainly did not retrieve them each morning with the intention of creating a book. The purpose of each poem was only to bring me back to myself, or to hold on to a moment I did not want to forget. Once I gave myself permission to rest more after that initial burnout, and once I stopped grinding toward the next accomplishment, the poems came on their own, little by little in fits and starts: effortless effort.

I've spent a lot of time over the past few decades trying to force poems into being. But I decided there would be none of that from now on. All I had to do was show up for whatever wanted to come, even if it seemed like nothing at first, recalling that this daily scrawling in a notebook is not work so much as a steady source of joy for me, a way to preserve everyday experiences that leave me with a quieter sense of awe. In other words, as I took my own sweet time and emerged from the spell of busyness, as I let myself feel the still-fresh sorrow of losing my mother so suddenly, I began writing just for myself again, which I see as the purest and most necessary creative intention. In fact, I hope that these poems might help you to unlock some of your own moments, that you'll be called to write in response to them, reflecting on your own relationship with rest. I encourage you to keep a notebook nearby, just in case you want to borrow a line and follow your own thread.

In life and on the page, I try to live by the wise words of Vietnamese Buddhist monk Thích Nhất Hạnh: "Have no expectations, and you will never be disappointed." May these poems remind you, as they have reminded me, that presence and wonder are often available to us, even in the most ordinary moments. May they show you, as they have shown me, that how we live and everything we do count as spiritual practice. Even the simple act of watering houseplants, if fully inhabited, can bring us deep peace and help us breathe more easily again.

PART ONE

All the Air You Can Breathe

Breathing Room

There should be a room in every house
or office building set aside strictly
for breathing. No speaking allowed,
no phones, clocks, or other devices
may be brought inside. Let the walls
be empty and white, only potted ferns
stirring near windows thrown open
to a night-breeze bearing the scents
of jasmine and lilac. You can count
if you like until your heartbeat slows
to its own natural pace, and your mind's
as blank as a page in the back of a book.
If someone asks for directions, say
it's the room at the end of the hall
with nothing else in it but a few plants
and all the air you can breathe.

Becoming Peace

Sometimes, when the house breathes
on its own, and I stare out the window
without purpose, in love with loneliness,
all of my moments—past, present,
and future—merge into one. And I see
among hummingbirds, moths, and bees
a pair of goldfinches, each of which
rests on the bobbing head of a zinnia,
tiny feet clinging as they peck away petals
to get at the center of the flower, where
they must sense some sweetness
waits just for them.

Waiting for Coffee

I could have lived in that moment forever
standing in line at the crowded café,
early risers huddled at their tables
with the burnt-toast scent of roasting coffee
wafting in the air around us. When my husband
turned to face me, opened his arms
in a wide bear hug and held me like that
for a single beat, heart to heart pulsing beneath
our coats and several layers of flannel
like we were the only two men in the universe.
Then it was over, and I stared up at burlap
sacks of beans stacked on the counter,
the ponytailed barista pulling shots
like nothing had happened, though I was
glowing when we stepped forward to order,
still held in the field of that sudden embrace.

Waiting for You

I am waiting for you to come home,
steeping in silence and sunshine
as my tea has soaked in hot water
long enough to become something new,
a different self. Shadow of a woodpecker
climbing a dead tree, and the dying
light held in the arms of swaying pines.
If I had my whole life to do over,
I'd still make all the same mistakes
because each one brought me closer
to you. Now I listen for the crunch
of gravel beneath tires and the slamming
of the car door before you glance up,
smiling at the window where I stand,
watching you walk toward me
all over again.

Thank You for Everything

Walking the roads after a snowstorm,
he put out an arm to stop me
as three deer streamed down the hill,
then kept holding me back
as two more morphed from trunks
and tree limbs into the lithe bodies
that leapt to follow the others back
into the woods. When we stepped
gingerly toward the place where they
had crossed, I was ready to start
talking again, until he asked,
"Do you smell them?" and I said
I did, now with a name for the rank
musk that hung in the air around us,
what I'd thought must just be
crushed pine needles, the scent
of churned-up soil. Having forgotten
whatever it was we were discussing—
a problem at work, bills to pay,
some politician's latest lies—

I remembered what the Japanese
Zen master Sono used to say
hundreds of years ago to anyone
who came to her in search of healing.
Each day, she told them, repeat:
"Thank you for everything, I have
no complaints whatsoever."

Grounded

The stories all forget that the Buddha
was just a man sitting beneath a tree
in the middle of the night, weathering
the storm of his thoughts and fears,
each one demanding: *Who do you think*
you are? His simple answer: to reach
down and touch the earth, feel the wet
hair of the grasses, the smooth skin
of sandy soil beneath his hand. And so
I say to myself: Ground yourself here.
Pick up a single dead oak leaf, if that's
all you can do, and turn it this way
and that, so the leathery surface gleams
in thin winter light, so that the earth,
which you are, can welcome you back.

After Despair

The sun still rose today
as it always has, striking
the snaking arms of our geranium
and lighting each wide leaf,
the heat seeming to make them
more pungent as I brushed past,
lifting all the window shades.
Outside, the slick brown leaves left
clinging to oaks shone at dawn
like sheets of hammered copper
that rattled in the slightest wind.
There were no more tears for me
today, though I shook my head
and asked myself, *What now?*
as I poured the boiling water
over coffee grounds in the filter
and leaned closer to breathe in
the fragrant steam, more grateful
than ever for the pleasure
of such simple things.

You, Too, Are Held

When I say the words *I'm grateful,*
it's like stepping into a house where
light spills out on the frosted grass,
and a fire crackles in the woodstove,
blue flames leaping up like laughter.
It's a place that always welcomes me
with shelves well stocked for winter—
jars of strawberry jam and peaches
swimming in syrup, a freezer filled
with sweet corn, and all the potatoes
I can eat asleep for now in the cellar.
I'm grateful, I say again, and it's like
slipping my hand into the open space
of my husband's, his fingers curling
around mine, or like placing my palm
over my heart before bed to remind
that tireless muscle starved of touch:
you, too, are held here in gratitude.

Like a Small Animal

I don't know how the heart goes
cold as an unpicked apple clinging
to the branch, encased in layers
of ice. Yet even the slightest gesture
can warm it, as if some hand were
reaching out to hold the hard skin,
melt off the months of bitterness.
Maybe a friend hugs you longer
than she needs to, just a few more
seconds of pressing you closer until
you want to live inside that gesture,
inhaling her perfume for the rest
of your life. Or a lover makes you
a turkey sandwich one day for lunch
with butter-crunch lettuce, pickles,
and extra mayo, and eating it at work
later, relishing every bite, you feel
that stirring in your chest, like a small
animal coming out of a long sleep,
blinking its tender eyes awake.

Relish

There is almost no difference
between *relish* and *release*
since what pleases us
can also free us,
if we pay enough attention—

scent of a chicken roasting
in the Crock-Pot,
water beaded on the glass lid,

and the tarp over the woodpile
whipping in autumn wind,
rippling and crackling
in anticipation
of all the fires to come.

Then there is the absence
that is also pleasure—
the silent phone on the table
whose screen stays black,

so the day becomes
like an empty bowl
scrubbed out and placed
on the dish drain,

the kitchen so quiet now
I can hear every drop of water
leaking from the faucet.

REFLECTIVE PAUSE

Like an Empty Bowl

Days off are excellent times to practice being present, giving our attention to whatever we find around us. But we have to fight our tendency to fill the free hours with tasks that do not feed us in larger ways. Some of us may not have entire days, and might have only a few minutes to ourselves, but this is still enough time to find that empty bowl feeling, when we can let go of what we want to happen, and what we think we need to do to be the perfect mother, father, husband, wife, daughter, son, worker, or friend. The poem "Relish" came to me on such a day, when I had a few hours before my husband was supposed to come home, but was having trouble focusing on a single thing. I had worked hard that week, so I decided I would just relish the simplicity of washing dishes, roasting a chicken for dinner, seeing what I could notice about these chores I typically think of as boring. After a full week of frenzied time in my life, I find it hard to release the restless energy that still courses through me. It is in these moments, as I know from my own experience, that we often reach for something we believe will give us relief from the leftover energy we don't know how to hold. Yet I try to bear in mind what Kierkegaard once wrote: "Anxiety is the dizziness of freedom." If we let anxious feelings slowly dissipate, they can eventually give way to more creative thinking and healthy action. But sitting still with discomfort takes patience. We must learn again to take pleasure in small things, in the wide open space of mind that sudden calmness or silence can bring.

INVITATION FOR WRITING & REFLECTION:

Sit alone in a room in your home, for however long you can manage. Look around and listen for several minutes. Using all of your senses, see what you notice that seems new to you, and then start writing: "I relish, I relish, I relish," listing all the small things that bring you joy. Try to let each sight, sound, or sensation speak to you, and see how space slowly gathers around it.

Finding the Islands

Look for islands of brief relief,
open spaces in an otherwise crowded day
where you can come ashore for a while,
find safe harbor. Hear again the warble
of hidden birds, and isolate each inter-
woven strand of song, even if you can't
name the small bodies that sing them.
Click the airplane icon on your phone,
which means no messages will fly to you
with their bad news, landing in the branches
of your mind. Let your thoughts climb
to the sky like the vines of morning glory,
and see the glint of a red pebble in the yard
still stippled with dew—the first wild
strawberry of the season, which you pluck
and eat right there in knee-high weeds,
tiny feast of an instant before the rest
of the day's worries try to haul you
back out to stormy seas.

Small Moments

The world is not made only of sorrow
and heartbreak. Something often
slips through the gaps of a given day—
dew, for instance, clinging to blades
of grass newly risen from the lingering
sleep of winter, those droplets soaking
your boots and the legs of your jeans
as you pass through, as proof that you
are here, and belong to this planet.
If that's not enough, then I give you
buttered sourdough toast smeared
with as much strawberry jam as that
bread can hold, and the first bite
whose burst of summer returns you
to the body, where small moments
like these are stored, like nutrients
leaves pull from the sun as soon
as it breaks through storm clouds,
filling the cracks with gold.

Kintsugi Again

In the Japanese art of mending ceramics
with powdered gold, no one ever
talks about how they'd leave the pots,
cups, and cracked bowls broken
for a while, sometimes whole generations.
And so I say to you: Let your heart stay
shattered in your chest, let it ache.
Some might claim you've now been
broken open, and can let in the light.
This might be true, but before you rush
to gloss over the wounds, filling
the holes with gold so they glimmer,
try to find beauty in the broken places too,
proof of where the fire left its marks on you.

Safe Space

When there is nowhere else you feel safe,
and you think that goodness has gone extinct;
when the world seems cold as a snowed-in car
that won't start anymore—step inside this poem.
Find solace in the spaces between each line,
breathe peace in the pause between words.
Let no one ever say you don't belong here—
you were born, you're alive, you exist: take this
as proof that you, too, are loved. Say this to yourself
until it is true: May I be safe, may all beings
on this planet be safe. And feel how a small fire
kindles in your chest, spreading to the bundle
of tinder that is your heart, still humming
its tireless, ancient hymn: *I am, I am, I am.*

Words Have Wings

Perhaps all that goes unspoken
lives in the back of the throat,
scratching at the sides, yearning
to be brought out—not as a cough
or cloud of shapeless breath,
but as a burst of the clearest words,
like a flock of swifts streaming
one after another from the mouth
of a chimney, filling the sky
with the sound of a thousand
tireless wings.

Whispers

Whispers live inside the body,
in tiny open spaces like the gaps
between rocks out of which pours
the sweetest spring water you have
ever tasted. If only you'd kneel,
search, find the source, the whispers
would tell you which way to turn,
when to stop, and what you need
in words as ancient as the air
that flows out of caves. You could
make a whole map of your life
just by sitting still and listening
until the small voice becomes
like a song you've been singing
since long before you were born.

How to Listen

Listening is a form of worship,
but you don't have to kneel
on the floor with folded hands
or mouth the perfect prayer.
Just open the door of yourself
to another, become the space
they step through to show you
who they are. This is holiness:
two people seated together
on the pew of a park bench,
at the altar of a kitchen table.
Even if no one says a word
for a while, receive the silence
until it's like a new language
only the two of you can speak.

Church

When I ask how you are,
imagine a field of untouched snow
stretching blank between us,
waiting for the answer of your steps—
perhaps hesitant at first, then
more certain as you begin to share
the sorrows and joys that sit
like unwrapped offerings
on the altar of your heart.

Here, there is time for you to say
all the words that have weighed
you down, hidden in the body
for years like unasked prayers.
No matter how far apart we stand,
I promise to listen for as long
as you need, in this open-air church
we enter together whenever
we agree to speak of deeper things.

Friendship

Please sit beside me
even when you'd rather be
anywhere else but here.
Say the wrong thing, as I
have no doubt said or done
the wrong thing to you.

We'll practice forgiving
each other as the tree
forgives the battering storm
that tears away its leaves,
at the same time sending
much-needed rain to roots.

Isn't friendship the crack
that lets light flood a room,
love pouring in from where
you'd least expect it,
through the smallest opening
of care between two people?

Missing Piece

I found something lost this morning
when I lay next to you on the couch
in a patch of winter sun finally breaking
over the mountains. I had not let myself
just be with you in so long—we were
like the silhouettes of boats passing by
each other at night on a river, both of us
too busy with our rowing to look up.
But as I leaned in, pressed my cheek
against your striped wool pajama top,
I saw you clearly, inhaling the clean
scent of your hair, and burying my face
in your chest until there was no space
between us.

Between Us

As I held the heft of his head in my hand,
kissing him once again before bed last night,
this time the weight and substance of his body
made me relish every sensation of our lips
pressing against each other, my palm cupping
the nape of his neck for a few seconds more
before I let go, and he lay back on his pillow.
Why do we forget that every human being
contains galaxies we'll never fully explore,
or lose sight of the miracle of two people
coming together to make something new,
intertwining their lives like the strands
of a rope made stronger by the braiding?
In that dark room softened by streetlamps,
I watched the silhouette of his form settle
beneath the sheets, facing me, but with eyes
now closed as I lay next to him, pretending
to read, pretending the world hadn't just
ripped open a little, light rushing through
that luminous seam.

Spiritual

It all counts as practice—
the way you stack clean dishes
in the drainer so they won't break,
how you wipe down the counter
and fold the towels. How you talk
to a co-worker, or your husband
after a hard day, saying to him:
You can lay your head in my lap, then
spending the rest of the evening
rubbing his temples to release all
the pain locked inside. And isn't this
as sacred an act as bowing to a statue
of the Buddha, or standing in line
for hours just to touch the worn
bronze toe of St. Peter in Rome,
believing that single gesture might
bless the rest of your life?

REFLECTIVE PAUSE

The Gift of Presence

I can sometimes forget that the whole point of spiritual practice—which for me includes meditation, prayer, and writing—is to live our moments with more presence, finding the sacred in the ordinary all around. As Naomi Shihab Nye has said of the act of writing: "Your life is the poem." What we practice or create is not separate from how we spend our time or how we hold the simple tasks, chores, and connections that make up a life. I wrote this poem after a period of deep fatigue and burnout, when I was in the process of returning to the gift of everyday life, after spending so many hours on planes, traveling back and forth across the country for work. I expected to be relieved when I arrived back home, but instead found myself depressed, overtaken with a tiredness that left me fearful for my health. Eventually, I realized that I needed to embrace the simplicity of life again, and find the holiness right here—washing dishes, folding laundry, rubbing my husband's head after a long day of work. It was around this same time that I learned about pilgrims who still kiss or touch the foot of a statue of St. Peter when they visit the Vatican, so much that the bronze toes have worn away and lost their definition. If some of us can believe a single gesture like that might bless the rest of our lives, can't we also believe the same of those things we touch and use as we move through our routines, letting every small thing bring us back home to the soul?

INVITATION FOR WRITING & REFLECTION:

What are some of the ordinary chores and acts that might count as spiritual/creative practice for you right now? You might describe a time when you saw that what you were doing in any given moment was just as much a form of worship as kneeling in church, sitting on a meditation cushion, or folding your hands in prayer. Feel free to begin with my first line, "It all counts as practice," and see what comes.

PART TWO

The Altar of a Moment

Ode to Boredom

Boredom is the blessing
that places me here
at the kitchen table,
where I see a single
yellow bud bursting
on the forsythia outside,
and a few of the white
blossoms of bloodroot
flaring up in leaf litter
despite the snow that
buried us this morning.
What task or chore
could be more important
than sitting still with
this emptiness, which
fills up as steadily
as a bowl left beneath
a leaky faucet, drop
by slow drop, until
a sudden happiness
ripples across the
surface of my life.

Wildflower

I want to guard the bright center
of my own life like the wide leaves
of bloodroot, one of the first wildflowers
to appear in the now-thawing earth.
How the leaves curl around the filament
of a stem, then the white bud that soon
forms at the tip, protecting it
from pelting sleet, from wind and rain
the way a palm will curve to cup
the rush of match-flame, keeping it lit.
This life is no small thing, though made
of the slightest gestures, and fading
faster than we'd like. It takes effort
to own the strength and fragility needed
to keep the inner fire going, no matter
the outer weather. See how bloodroot
blossoms and trembles in the same instant
like a lantern flickering in its dark corner
of the forest path, here to light the way
for as long as it can.

How We Heal

This is how we heal, one cell
at a time, drawing in the nutrients
and air offered to the body,
which rejoices in stillness
as the maple celebrates a pummeling
rain in spring, even the patches
of lichen on its branches and trunk
glowing greener in the meager light
of dusk. We heal by asking
for what we need from the ground
we stand on, roots reaching out—
calling, speaking to others moving
in their own slow-motion way
toward the wholeness that is this
leafing out from tight red buds
whose blush you can barely see
at first, like color rising up,
returning to the face.

Self-Care

Some days it feels like a foreign language
I'm asked to practice, with new words
for happiness, work, and love. I'm still learning
how to say: a cup of tea for no reason,
what to call the extra honey I drizzle in,
how to label the relentless urge to do more
and more as *useless*. And how to translate
the heart's pounding message when it comes:
enough, *enough*. This morning, I search for words
to capture the glimmering sun as it lifts
above the mountains, clouds already closing in
as fat droplets of rain darken the deck.
I'm learning to call this stillness self-care too,
just standing here, as goldfinches scatter up
from around the feeder like broken pieces
of bright-yellow stained-glass, reassembling
in the sheltering arms of a maple.

We Are Miracles

It's not easy becoming
something new. Look at the leaves
locked tight in their buds,
which form long before spring,
waiting out ice storms and snowfall
to unfurl the flags of their
true selves into a roof of green.
We think it must be simple,
changing with each new season,
yet fear and doubt still fill
even the widest leaves of the maple,
at last learning to turn light
into sugar, unaware as they shiver
there at the tip of a branch
of the miracles they've now become.

You Belong

Step out and breathe in the fog
that smudges this summer morning.
Touch the hot-pink petals
of echinacea studded with droplets,
each of which contains whole planets
you will never set foot on.
Know that you also hold many worlds
unseen inside you, as do
the tiny leopard frogs who leap up
out of the way when you walk
through the grass. Let the wet blades
stroke your legs, soak your sandals,
and call each shiver evidence
of your aliveness, proof that you, too,
belong on the earth.

After Grief

We forget that spring comes
not all at once, in one
wide sweep of warmth
and green blanketing the ground,
but blossom by blossom,
and blade by blade,
beginning with a single
crocus creaking open
the hinges of its petals
in the chill darkness
before dawn one morning,
having sensed the barest
hint of sun still buried
like a bulb beneath
the horizon, and decided
that's all the proof
it needs to say its own
small yes to life
in this new season.

Why We Say Yes

Because it's like a rusted-shut door
opens in the chest with each yes,
and life can finally pass through—
the breeze scented with diesel
from a tractor several fields away,
and the first lilacs in a neighbor's yard
welcoming this sun-struck season
with constellations of violet blooms
you lean deeper into, closing your eyes
and breathing in, the whole body
becoming the answer to a question
asked by each new moment:
Will you, will you?

The First Peony

Soon, the rain-slicked bud will be
nothing more than a memory
for the plant, and for me, having
held it in my hand on this gray
May morning, when I looked out
and couldn't resist stepping across
wet mulch and clover to get closer,
to touch the pink seam through which
petals were already bursting to become
something far more extravagant
than necessary—beauty as its own
reason for being. Haven't you, too,
felt the pull toward some brief
opulence, born not out of ignorance
but full awareness of these limited,
time-bound bodies? Doesn't it feel
like the creaking open of a tiny door
the moment the peony finally
chooses to bloom?

To See You Blooming

I want to tell the child in you:
You will never be too much for me.
No matter what I say or do, I want
to see you blooming like the flowers
you spent countless hours planting
and tending in the yard, a riot of color
and tangle of green reaching up and out
of themselves to be seen, to be felt.
I want you to expose the passion
you spent your childhood trying to hide.
I want you to open like the echinacea,
showing a heart-center full of seeds
no one knew were held in the roots,
so much potential for creation revealed
without an ounce of shame or doubt.

How to Let Go

Let go of who you think you are
and sink back into the bareness of being,
as fat white flakes paper down
from a sky crowded with clouds. See how
the dried-out husks of coneflowers
hold their burden of snow, letting it
slide off like an old name, or a habit
that no longer fits. Every flower in winter
becomes a crown of seeds, blossom
of pure potential in these coldest months.
Just as you are a collection of moments,
each one as blank as the snow now
blanketing the yard, waiting to be changed
by the imprint of every step you take.

Choices

You can grieve the leaves stripped
from the maple, all that empty
space between bare branches,
or you can bless the abundance
of light shining through, buffing
the pine boards of the floor until
they turn the color of clover honey.
You can mourn the coneflowers
now shriveled and brown, say
the whole world's gone to ruin,
or you can stand at the window
watching the lively yellow blossom
of a goldfinch feasting on each
crown of seeds, sending more than
a few back home, down into
the open ground, which knows
how to receive them.

REFLECTIVE PAUSE

Moments of Hope

When we give ourselves the space and rest we need, we begin to see that we have a choice: We can curse our current circumstances, or we can appreciate and accept exactly where we are. This might include a whole spectrum of emotions—the sudden sweep of sorrow or the swoop of anger through us or the blessing of joy. Often, we create a false separation in our minds between these feelings, as if they can't coexist, sometimes arising in the same moment of deep presence. We can try to make space for all that comes up in us, so that we embrace the pleasures that arrive as well, even as we curse the suffering in other parts of our lives and the world. We can grieve our losses, and the larger losses of the human family, even as we welcome the abundance of light on a sunny day, shining through bare trees. I have always felt that we turn to poetry during difficult times precisely because poems are such small but spacious containers that hold so much with just a few powerful details. They can hold our bliss, our pain, our awe. On the day I describe here, I was walking on a trail in the woods near our house, cursing the pain I was feeling as I suffered through a bout of shingles. Then the sun suddenly came out, spilling across the forest floor the very color of clover honey. I felt the instant release of wonder for a world that still manages to stun me. Because so many emotions and thoughts rise up in us at once, perhaps our choice rests in which ones we focus on, which ones we allow to guide us through this singular life we've been given. And when we can care for ourselves even in the smallest of ways, it becomes easier to welcome such moments of hope.

INVITATION FOR WRITING & REFLECTION:

Write about a time when it occurred to you that you have a choice between grief and abundance, resistance and joy. How did it feel to be torn between two co-arising emotions? You might begin in the same spirit as my poem here, writing, "You can grieve . . ." with the idea that there's always a choice in what we allow to lead us forward.

Messengers

Hope slips into the house unannounced
like seeds that cling to my husband's jeans
when he comes home from the farm fields,
cottony fluff of milkweed and thistle,
and seed-heads of rye grass all drifting
across the mudroom floor into every corner,
waiting among ribbons of old cobwebs
to be swept up later, taken back outside.
It's the way of the world, life biding its time
until it finds that one chance in a billion
and bursts into some wild new version of itself
that lived inside from the very start.
Like the puffball mushrooms we brush past
while harvesting the last of the Brussels sprouts,
how they send out spores at the slightest touch,
countless messengers rising up around us
in a cloud of rich smoke, riding the gust
of every breath we take.

Hope Watches

Hope watches from the window
like a small child waiting
for his parents to come home.

His eyes are the lights
hope keeps burning
long into the night, even when

it seems no one will return.
Hope breathes on the glass,
asks each of us to write our name,

leave some sign that we were here,
that we cared enough
to keep searching.

Stay

Stay with this. There is no escape.
Though your heart aches, and the world's
shrunk to the size of these few rooms,
though fear plucks the strings of each nerve,
and you want nothing more than to burst
free of the casing of your own mind, like
a bittersweet berry giving its softer self
to overwintering birds—still, dawn-light
breaks blue above the swaying maples,
and the space heater kicks on, steaming
windows with its warm, constant breath.
Stay with this, and it will pass through
like a sudden storm whose sole purpose
is to scatter leaves, seeds, and spores—
each to find a new home. Though wind
cuts terribly against the skin of your face
as you press on, remember it will calm
and cease, but not before hauling off
all that you no longer need.

Wick

There are times in life when a brief
darkness must fall. We can let it
steal over us, yet feel no shame,
recalling the slow way dawn chases
night from the kitchen, inch by inch
extinguishing shadows around
the kettle, and burners on the stove
with their hidden rings of blue flame,
and the curved faucet with its silver
braid of water filling a glass for the first
sip of a new day. Yes, there will be
singing in the dark times, but the music
will live inside us as we learn to keep
the fraying wick always lit.

Flicker

What a small flicker is given

To each of us to know.

—Naomi Shihab Nye

You go around all day guarding the flicker
you found again that morning. Cupping a hand
to protect it from wind, holding it close
to the chest, so no wayward breath blows it out.
This flame, shaky and uncertain, is how you
light the rooms behind your eyes that no one
has ever seen. The wick may be frayed,
and the wax will last for just an hour or two
at best, but it is enough. It will always be
enough to look into the eyes of another
and pass the flicker on to them.

Folding Altar

I carry my church with me
wherever I go, unfolding the altar
of a moment while out walking
with my husband, pausing to pick
a few dandelions gone to seed,
taking a deep breath, then blowing,
sending those silver messengers
into the air above a field,
each one the seed of a prayer
I say every day I'm alive:
Please let me give up all hope
for a better past, and just be here
by the side of the driveway,
watching wisps of clouds turning
pink with evening, then purple,
and listening to the complex solo
of a catbird perched in a maple
as we say goodbye to the light,
which may leave the sky tonight
but will stay with us, flickering
for years to come.

Everything That Is Divided

Everything that is divided, split,
must eventually reveal the softness
at its center, like milkweed pods
that seem dead at the edge of winter,
the fluff of a seed still clinging
like hope—no, like faith to the stem
of a plant that knows it will go on,
this is not the end of the story,
even if those days of monarchs
and blossoms filled with nectar
and caterpillars feasting on leaves
are over for now. The plant has
learned to see the possibility in each
small thing we offer to the world.

REFLECTIVE PAUSE

Seeds of Possibility

None of us knows what the future will hold, and if we feel exhausted and drained, it remains difficult for us to consider what comes next. When in a place of burnout, or hunkered down in sorrow, we forget that—like the earth in winter—we are entering our own transitional phase, a threshold moment of great possibility. In my own grief journeys, having lost my father at the age of twenty, and my mother more recently, I have learned to allow myself fallow periods when little can be accomplished, perhaps even nothing substantial. I believe we need times like these in each day, month, and season of our life—short and long stretches of rest and recharge, so that we can return more nourished to a life of intention. This agreement not to do much when we can, to let ourselves feel useless and even hopeless for a while, may be necessary, but it can feel like a kind of death to the life that was. With each new conscious breath we take, with each hour or minute we give to ourselves, free from outer distractions, we start to see the softness at the center of everything. Perhaps we become softer with ourselves as well. We begin to trust that every small, kind thing we offer to the world contains the seed of so much beauty and strength, it can't help but ripple out, touching so many unknown lives. I often think of these lines from May Sarton's poem "A Thought": "Brute power/is not superior/to a flower." We cannot simply force or power our way through a difficult time. Instead, we can become like a flower that has gone to seed and softened completely, having agreed to embrace the rest that will help it grow in spring.

INVITATION FOR WRITING & REFLECTION:

Where do you find evidence of softness revealed right now, at a time when things might seem hard and even lifeless? What small things have you offered to yourself and the world lately that plant the seeds of possibility, and the promise of more light to come?

PART THREE

The Light That Lives in Us

The Promise

Barely ten degrees this morning,
yet we heard the liquid trill
of red-wing blackbirds perched
at the top of a still-bare maple
wearing only the blush of buds
guarding their green. Just a few
hints of that headlong song,
and we stopped loading the car,
laid down the canvas grocery bags
to yell and point up at them—
and then they were gone. But not
the promise they left with us
and planted beneath the layers
of iced-over snow gleaming at dawn:
You will make it through this.

And how did I hear, contained
in those ancient notes, the water
of running brooks, the shimmer
of rivers we'll soon dive into again,
baptism and risk? How did I hear
the swelling and deepening pink
of sakura cherry tomatoes plucked
from dusty vines and feasted on
in the fields, while the tireless light
keeps singing across our skin?

November Sunrise

We now know the human body glows
if placed in total darkness,
our skin emitting a light so faint
the naked eye can't begin to discern it.
But I don't need scientists or
research studies this morning to see
how dawn-light—now yellow, now pink,
now violet—arcs across the bay
and bathes our faces as we stare out.
We've turned off every light in the house
so we don't miss a bright instant
of this November sunrise—now the pure
gold of alchemists' dreams rising
casually over the tree-lined horizon
and making a path toward us across
the ocean as if we could walk
on water to meet the light that also
lives in us.

Hello, Little Sun

On the rusty tin roof of a red barn
in rural Quebec, someone has carved
the words, *Bonjour, petit-soleil*—
Hello, little sun—and I read them
while passing by as if this message is
meant for me, as if I need reminding
that delight gives off its own brightness
and heat inside the body, like a tiny
star we carry with us wherever we go,
whether driving home under the soft
blue dome of the northern sky, or standing
in line at a market in the city center,
an old man counting out coins to pay
for his cup of black coffee on the counter,
then saying goodbye to the cashier
in such slow and careful French,
I can feel the warmth of every word.

Forgiveness

Overnight, in a matter of hours,
forgiveness descends like a light
dusting of snow that coats everything—
each blade of grass and quiet car,
each jagged branch covered in a thin
film of blankness and possibility. Now,
your footsteps are met with softness,
the rest of your life like the unwritten
chapter of a novel in which you find
at last the kind of love that allows you
to stand in the yard just after dawn,
marveling at the transformation, as if
someone had flipped a switch marked
Gentleness, marked *Compassion*, and now
you carry that light with you.

How To Be Alone

Wait long enough, and the sting of loneliness
you can hardly stand turns into something
a little sweeter, like a gentle animal
dozing at your feet, going where you go
and nuzzling your hand with the kind
of unconditional love we believe is reserved
only for others. Turn to the ordinary
objects of your life—the coffee cup's rim
stained with joy, the favorite hoodie
fraying at the elbows, the lumpy pillow
that knows the shape of your dreams exactly.
The world tells stories you can hear
only when you decide not to run away
from the pain that is your birthright,
when you decide to sit by yourself tonight
for as long as you can, unwrap the wounds
and let it all pass through.

Small, Good Things

Tonight, the fireflies blinking on

and off as light leaves the sky

are the synapses of my skin

firing as a breeze blows past me.

I sit on the porch steps doing nothing

for the few minutes I allow myself,

letting all the small, good things

from the day gather and hover

like mosquitoes landing with a

tremble among the hairs on my arms.

Enough

What if we felt as complete
as the full moon tonight,
so wholly ourselves we cut
a hole through whatever
darkness tries to hide
our blinding-bright faces.

What if we gave our bodies
over to song as the cricket does,
not lamenting the end of summer
as we imagine, but calling out
to every other body hidden
among blades of grass, saying
to all who can hear: *I'm here.*

What if we loved ourselves

so fully we could shed the self

that no longer serves us

without an ounce of grief

like the moth splayed across

the window screen, whose wings

powder the night with tiny stars

as it flies, never once looking back.

The Spaces Between

for Carrie and Peter Sherrill

Learn to love what brings you space—
long car ride, eternity of flipping
through magazines in the waiting room,
the boredom of an August afternoon
when you notice a lime-green tree frog
asleep for hours outside the window.
How many minutes can you spend—
as if time were a limitless currency—
just watching his shut eyes for a flutter
of life, before you come back to the lists,
the news, an overseas flight, which
the airline canceled without telling you,
and find that you can breathe around
each worry, rest in the gaps between.

Finding God

for Kara Lawler

Find God in the spaces between—
the gap in a mossy stone wall
in which a chipmunk makes its home,
the sudden silence that brings
two people closer together until they
lock eyes and share the first kiss
of many thousands over the years.
Can you hear God speaking even now?
Not with words, but in the simple
lull of the evening when you look up
from washing lettuce in the sink
and see a hummingbird moth—half-
insect, half-animal—sipping nectar
from the clustered purple blooms
of a butterfly bush, each tiny flower
a doorway, each second of your
undivided attention another way
to enter the heaven right here.

What If

What if this is all we get of heaven,
little moments of joy sending out
their sharp scent like the basil plant
standing guard by the back door,
its leaves wanting nothing more
than to be torn, their essence released
to the night air. I can still make out
the jewel-like blooms of the purple
crown vetch crowding the flowerbed
around the stone, its vines once thought
to be invasive, though now we know
they nourish and restore even
the most depleted soil in the brief
time they come alive each summer.

What You Planted

In front of the garden you planted
so that I could trace the slow-motion
unfolding of daisies in soft mulch
you spread yourself, you also placed
a lopsided rock shaped like a heart
out of which the flowers now seem
to grow, as if they'd found the cracks
in the stone to rise through and bloom,
as your love has done in me, slipping
seeds into gaps and patches of soil
where I once believed no sunlight
or warmth would ever reach.

Why I Can't Stop Loving You

Because once, in the middle of a fight,
trading heated words back and forth
on the warming May air, you paused
and walked back to the side of the road
where you picked up a hawk feather
that even I in my righteousness
had to admit was a beautiful thing—
faded brown stripes across a creamy
white background, all the plumage
still smooth and intact, lost when
the red-tail lifted off, quick as my anger
that day after we came home, and I
watched you place the feather gently
on the bench in the hallway, as if it was
a matter of life and death, the way
you laid it down.

REFLECTIVE PAUSE

Beauty Is Its Own Excuse

We have all had our fair share of "human moments," times when we lose our temper and drop the thread of connection. On the morning I describe here, I had completely lost myself and was picking a fight with my husband because I felt anxious about something else. He was patient beyond reason, trying to listen and receive what I was saying without getting upset himself. But when he paused for just a few seconds to pick up a hawk feather, and then later, when he laid it down on the bench in our hallway with such tenderness and reverence, I felt my anger lift. Something about the physicality of his slow movements, and his ability to find beauty even in a moment of conflict, brought me out of the cloud of my own churned-up emotion, and back to the actual world—the gravel road on which we walked, the hawk that lost that elegantly shaped and smooth feather, the wooden bench where we sit each day to put on and take off our shoes. Out of the space of that unexpected perspective, I began to see how powerful it can be to pause in the middle of something, especially when we feel ourselves spinning out, losing control. We are often told to take a breath, and while that can be helpful, perhaps the most useful thing we can do when caught in the swirl of emotions is to find a way to rest in the moment again. Maybe we can notice our physical surroundings, and find something beautiful or striking to pick up and hold in our hand. The whole experience reminded me of what Ralph Waldo Emerson once wrote, "Beauty is its own excuse for being." And beauty is perhaps the best excuse to let ourselves pause, even when that's the last thing we want to do.

INVITATION FOR WRITING & REFLECTION:

Describe an experience that lifted you out of whatever difficult emotion you were feeling at the time. What bit of beauty have you found lately that is its own excuse for being, that was worth stopping everything to appreciate? How might you cultivate moments of brightness like this more often for yourself?

Cardinal

Be someone's cardinal
glimpsed between leaf-shadows,
flit of brightness so startling
they have to blink to believe their eyes.
Be the reason someone looks up
from the cracked blankness of concrete
and remembers the world
is so much larger than what's locked
inside head and heart. Be the red
swoop from tree to tree, the thread
that stitches one uncertain
moment to the next.

Held

Today, what's keeping me together
seems as thin as the strand
of old cobweb strung between
two rubbery leaves of the jade plant.

I watch it tremble and stretch
with each breath of breeze
barely blowing through the window,
and marvel that it doesn't break

but instead dances in the wind—
empty clothesline, high wire
able to withstand only the smallest
of bodies, the lightest touch.

Perhaps what looks most fragile
from a distance only grows stronger
as it's tested. Maybe we're all
made of such invisible threads

somehow holding each other up.

Kinship

Don't you feel it some mornings
before the words of news stories
and headlines take over the mind—
this kinship with all things
humming in the quieter air
around chipmunk and vole, near
crocus bloom and old fence post
whose rusted barbed wire
has buried itself in tree trunks,
and can no longer harm?
Even the tiny newts you move
out of the road and the woolly bear
caterpillar using its whole body
to cross to the other side
seem to hold some silent glow.

Don't you find it especially
with your neighbor, whose
bumper sticker and yard signs
suggest he believes things
bewildering to you, whose face
still fills with light when he
sees you passing by, and shakes
your hand, his bare palm so warm
and soft against your own?

Try Softer

Honor wherever you are,
whether the door to your life
has blown off its hinges,
or you find the simplest joy
sitting in a patch of winter sun
on that corner of the carpet
where you love to stretch.
Try softer, not harder—
giving yourself a safe place
to land your attention, resting
in this threshold moment
through which wind, snow,
and light all enter alike.

REFLECTIVE PAUSE

This Threshold Moment

We have all at some point been told—or told ourselves—to try harder. And we know how that pressure feels inside the body, urging us to shut down our own emotions, our intuition. Lately, I have been trying to ask myself the central question of this poem: What would it mean to *try softer*, holding life with more generosity and calm? Often, my poems will bloom out of a first line whose message I need to hear, and the poem "Try Softer" came out of the blue, in a voice that did not sound entirely like my own. "Honor wherever you are" is another way of saying that we must name and accept—even embrace, if we can—the river of feeling that flows through each of us in this moment. We might feel tired and unwell, unable to fulfill the simplest of chores or obligations. Many times, however, it's not until we give in fully to our limitations that we begin to feel the slight lift of relief. In a culture that values hardness and constant productivity, we are each called to bring more tenderness to all of our interactions, especially in how we treat ourselves. The poet Jane Hirshfield has said: "Tenderness does not choose its own uses. It goes out to everything equally." When we commit to trying softer, a gentler form of attention spreads out, touching every person and object we encounter. We become a kind of threshold, letting it all in, and letting it all out, hopefully with the same kindness we can now offer ourselves.

INVITATION FOR WRITING & REFLECTION:

What would it mean for you to "honor wherever you are"? You might write that phrase at the top of the page, and see what images or memories come to you to describe such a radical but necessary openness toward the ordinary wonders of daily life.

PART FOUR

These Commonplace Miracles

Blue-Eyed Grass

All spring long, you have waited
for the tiny star-shaped flowers
of the blue-eyed grass, glancing
out the window, squinting at that
same place in the yard where they
appear each year. Why do we try
to rush delight, strong-arm joy
into busy lives, when so much
beauty already seeds itself beneath
our restless feet? Why not sit out
on the back porch and watch for
the moment these small beings
blink open their eyes, more violet
than blue in the late afternoon,
awakening some wildness
too long asleep in you?

Oregano

I kneel in the gravel outside our house
where a clump of oregano's somehow
grown, unlikely leaves I crush between
my fingers to release the scent that brings me
back into my body, this moment, my life.
This plant that no one planted, sprouted
from a seed that must have stowed away
in the muddy folds of my husband's jeans
to slip between stones, and make a home
here where water gathers after every storm.
I say yes to its sharp fragrance, greening
the autumn air around me, and breathe in
until I see how little it takes to fall in love
with the world again.

Dandelions

It is a risk, isn't it, to give your love
so completely to the hardy yellow heads
of dandelions you can't bring yourself
to pull up from the yard, leaving them
blazing like small stars around which unseen
worlds keep spinning. The petals arranged
in the shape of a crown so the flower can hear
bees and other pollinators as they fly near,
so it can, in those few slim instants, choose
to sweeten its nectar, making sure that
others learn of this sudden feast over which
you now hover, kneeling before the plant
some would call a weed, missing out on
these commonplace miracles dropped
like lucky pennies everywhere at our feet.

The Sweetness of Doing Nothing

Before the appointments, in spite of fatigue,
feel what the Italians call *dolce far niente,*
the sweetness of doing nothing. It's true,
you are still doing something as you pull on
boots and parka and trudge through snow
to the park for your usual two-mile loop.
But now you can move without expectation,
outside of the lines of your endless task list.
Hear the crunch of ice as you step into
the ghost-shapes of your old footprints
from yesterday. Feel your breath catch
in your throat as a red-tail hawk lifts off
from its perch on a bare branch choked
with bittersweet vines, each red berry
shriveled but gleaming, now trembling
with the hawk's startled movements,
talons letting go of what they'd held
so tightly just moments ago.

The Watched Hawk

Only the watched hawk—
the one I see now, startled
from his perch in a maple—
bares the white undersides
of his wings as he glides
between trees in the gloaming
over this autumn field,
darkness clinging to every part
of him except those pale,
soft feathers that flash
for an instant, then vanish
with him into the distance.

I might never have looked up
to catch the point of his beak
slicing through chilly air
or perked my ears to hear
his piercing, ancient cry
as it echoed across the sky,
and so I carry his presence
with me back inside like
a lit candle around which
I am cupping a hand to keep
the moment alive.

To Be Held

I want to be held by each moment
as a pond holds the spring peepers,
as water vibrates with that chorus
of craving that fills the April night.
I want to be held like the heavy blossom
of a trillium propped up by its stem,
and I want to bloom like that too—
slowly at first, sipping droplets of dew,
then fully alive to a warming world.
I want to be held like pollen stored
in the sacs of bumblebees, something
precious to carry home, as that buzzing
body holds its own sense of duty
and purpose, guided by its tireless
mission to visit every open flower
on the sun-dappled forest floor.

Walking Meditation

In the sudden cool of a summer morning,
I saw several of those soon-to-be newts
known as red efts huddled beneath
the blanket of a leaf. As slow-moving
as monks, they love to lounge in the middle
of forest trails on a cushion of moss
or on the warmer stones of a gravel road,
as if their sole purpose was to catch
our attention, ring the bell of the moment
with bright bodies more orange than red,
reminding us to watch where we walk.

Keep in Touch

A friend won't answer you anymore,
which may mean you aren't talking.
That job you applied for? No reply.
And you haven't heard from your own
family in over a week. But at least
the world is still speaking to you,
reaching out in all the ways it can
to keep in touch. Like this droning
cloud of mosquitoes and deer flies
hovering, wanting to kiss you
with a fervor reserved for lovers.
Or the slick rock you find sticking up
from the ground, somehow sweating
in the August heat, and giving off
a slight glint in tree-filtered light as you
place your hand against its cool face
and feel the transfer that happens—
how little it takes to shift a mood
in this communion of skin and stone.

A Question of Time

Where does the present moment go
when it leaves? Does it slip between
glimmers of light dancing through gaps
in the thinning canopies of trees?

Does it flow over rocks in the creek
light as a dust mote, catching on
a snag of oak leaves near the bank
where the water's begun to freeze?

Or does it drift into the open mouth
of an old beaver dam—little spark
in the dark—weaving itself once again
with the timeless silence inside?

REFLECTIVE PAUSE

Mindfulness Bells

Stillness of mind, which can be accessed by sitting still or even while running or walking, unlocks the timeless silence that already exists inside each of us. This is why we are nourished so much by outer silence, and why it allows us to enter the ever-fleeting present moment, when we can remember that it is right here. Yet silence is hard to come by these days, with the increasing noise of both the external world and our own minds, filled by news and a great deal of information we simply don't need. We do, however, need the present moment, no matter how quickly it seems to go, because the now—as most of us know—is all we ever really have. Perhaps it would help to imagine each moment as a living thing we must handle with care, like a spark in the dark or a small animal in need of our attention. Perhaps if we saw it as a portion of time that each of us was handed and tasked with tending for as long as it stays, we would not look past or ignore so many of our moments.

It can be helpful to pause in the middle of whatever we are doing simply to feel the quality of the present, so alive and dissolving at the same time into the next moment, and the next. We can also create what I call "mindfulness bells," little signals that occur throughout the day, reminding us to pause and breathe. A mindfulness bell might be a word you hear over and over at your office, a song you love to play, or a number that seems to appear over and over. It could be any sound or image that pulls you briefly out of the stream of thinking and back to the physical world around you. By stopping on my walk to listen for the red-wing blackbirds that have returned for spring, or feeling the scuff of my shoes on the carpet before a meeting, I enter a common center in which countless others are experiencing their own present moments with me throughout the world. In this way, I can live my moment fully before it goes.

INVITATION FOR WRITING & REFLECTION:

Think back to a time in your life when you felt deeply present and aware, but then the shimmering moment seemed to drift away, not to be recaptured. You might describe the specific details of this instance to a friend, or write about how it felt in your body, heart, and mind to be so present for a time.

Floaters

Soon after my mother's death,
I started to see these silver glimmers
in the air—reminders, visitations,
winks from the other side, or so
I told myself. Some might blame
aging, retinal floaters, a mind
responding to sudden loss, but I
wouldn't give them up for the world.
Earlier, washing my hands, I saw
one by the faucet where a tiny
spider had woven its web between
the soap dispenser and wall.
Just a flash where there was no sun,
no light turned on—then gone.
Like a signal fire that says to me:
Don't worry, I'm still alive somehow.

After Loss

Now you can make a temple anywhere
with the flickering candle of memory,
the hallowed ground of any patch of grass
or worn-out carpet where your loved one
once walked, alive and breathing.
Perhaps the fact that you can lose
someone so essential has shown you
the whole world is holy, worthy
of worship—the lopsided smile
of the cashier at the Home Depot,
the way she said, "That's okay, hon,"
when you apologized for your impatience.
Or the pint of strawberries on the table,
flecks of soil and straw still stuck
to gleaming skin, how the motion
of bringing one to your lips is closer
to prayer than any pair of folded hands.

At the Monastery

I join the others who fold their hands
and bow to a statue of the Buddha
as they enter and leave the temple.
But I want to ask: Would you bow
to the blown-apart peony, its petals
strewn like slips of silk in the grass
after last night's storm? Would you bow
to the miracle of your mother's voice
recorded and stored on your phone,
singing "Happy Birthday," as she did
each year before she died? What about
the honeybee, going about its business
of feeding the world simply by doing
the work it was given? And the crack
in the sidewalk that allows a few purple
asters to bloom and sway at the feet
of whomever passes by? What about
the humble pillow cradling your head
at night, faithful as any lover, learning
your shape, gently cupping the nape
of your neck?

You Are Here

I don't think we do enough bowing
to the simple things, the humble acts,
like sweeping dust and hair from the stairs
or wiping down the windows so I have
a clear view of that slim crimson strip
of the red-wing blackbird, first sign
of spring I could kneel and kiss. I bow
to the box of my mother's ashes, the way
grief stays evergreen yet still changes,
losing its needles and shedding limbs,
bending in wind I think will destroy me.
I bow to the blue Post-it note stuck
to my bedroom door, which says: *You have*
already arrived, you are here, the words
slowing the locomotive of my runaway
heart and mind each time I read them.

Nor'easter

I lie in bed this morning, worried
about the state of the world, when I turn
to find a pair of headlights slicing
through the predawn darkness at the end
of our driveway, and know my father-in-law
has come to plow us out after last night's
sudden snowstorm. *Bless you,* I say
to the cab of his truck, to his steady hands
on the wheel, marked by years of carpentry,
to cigarette smoke embedded in the seats
and steam curling up from the plastic lid
on his cup of gas station coffee. To this man
who loves us enough to make our house
his first stop, who can be counted on
even in the middle of another nor'easter
before the sun's a wink over the mountains,
lowering his plow-blade to scrape us a path
out into the hope of a brand-new day.

Little Hope

Some days, what we need
is a clean, hard rain to wash
away the world's troubles,
to pool in each crack of the
buckled sidewalk, the divots
of the newly mended street.
See how that fresh water
offers itself to drinking robins,
gives back the blue of sky
as if hope itself had gathered
in puddles overnight.

An Overcast Morning

Just hours before, you were sure
the sun would not shine today,
and here comes the light of dawn,
making the pale sky blue again,
angling through trees like a ladder
you could climb if you wanted to.
Now you see last night's raindrops
clinging to the tips of everything,
each bare limb or snapped-off twig
a glittering necklace, and the day
suddenly so generous, giving away
such riches for free.

Gathering

after Nina Bagley

I miss those days back when anything
I picked up became priceless and sacred—
a hunk of quartz glinting in the sun,
an old oak leaf dried to parchment,
a wild turkey feather snagged on a branch,
just waiting for me to pass by and claim it.
No matter that the leaf would turn to dust
and the feather lose all its softness
when stuffed in my pocket among sticks,
patches of moss, and the acorns I couldn't
live without. What do I keep now
that is so essential? Paper bills, plastic cards
that pretend to say who I am, the keys
to house and car. I remember my mother
making me lay it on the table before bed,
how the treasure I'd gathered came clattering
out of me—*All of it,* she said—evidence
of how rich I'd been for a single day.

When Feeling Lost

Sit alone by an open window
as rain-cooled wind tosses the trees,
scatters the white petals of viburnum
like your own useless worries
on soft mulch beneath. Hear how the air
carries the calls of newly fledged wrens
resting for now in a brush pile,
afraid to fly. Let peace swoop down
into your life, perch in the empty branches
of your lungs with each newborn breath.
Let stillness take your hand as when
you were a child, and they said,
if you're ever lost in the woods or confused
by a crowd, it helps to stay in one place—
not moving, doing nothing, so that you
may be found again.

The Leap

You could make the necessary change
right here and now, let all the old
dead bolts of doubt click open inside you.
Feel the doors swing wide as light
pours into the sky above the maples,
shining through that blue like stained-glass.
Isn't this moment just as sacred
as the next? Is there any such thing
as safety, or comfort that lasts? Step out
into wet grass at dawn, and see how
leopard frogs launch themselves
out of your path, trusting the muscles
of their own back legs to carry them,
not caring exactly where they end up
as long as they take the leap.

What the Heart Says

The mind may leap five steps ahead,
devices pinging with new messages,
alerts, alarms. But the heart says,
There is no emergency. That muscle
wanting to unclench, aching to flex
as free as the monarch nectaring
on a Mexican sunflower at the cusp
of autumn. Don't we all long for
space to pause and draw sweetness
from each bright thing in our path?
Don't we crave the slowness of that
butterfly perched on orange petals,
coming alive in a way it never can
while in mid-air, wings folding and
unfolding their own form of prayer?

The Only Prayer

Because there was nothing else to do,
and the news frightened me as usual,
I took a walk on my favorite trail
in the woods, and because the snow
began to melt as soon as it fell,
everything was wet—the lichen a bright
lime-green on the bark of each fallen tree,
the leaves beneath my feet deliciously
soft as they squelched and sank back
into the arms of the earth that shaped them.
I picked up one of the limp, gold-
toned beech leaves, pressed it to my chest,
then left my despair on a mossy trunk
and said the only prayer that matters:
I'm here, I'm here, I'm here.

Change

No matter how painful the change,
let yourself become a new creation.
Do you think the maples push out
their red buds each spring without
an ache in the skin of their limbs?
Do you think the marsh ferns unfurl
without effort, without missing the selves
they once were? Each frond like a newly
feathered wing reaching up into this
uncertain air we all breathe together.

As Breath Turns to Light

I breathe in anxiety, fear, everything
others want me to be—that black smoke—
and watch it turn to light with each exhale,
as I let it go into spacious air. I become
a filter for all that is harsh and difficult
in this world, and I hold on to none of it.
Like the hickories forming a green tunnel
over the road that leads to our house,
how they absorb the heat and make the light
that passes through their leaves seem softer,
kinder, as it falls across my face.

No Mud, No Lotus

This is the most radical thing you can do,
return to your roots, stay in the muck
and mud of the pond, feeling everything.
It's how the lotus grows, seeds germinating
underwater where others might drown,
stems curling slowly upward to reach
the surface, and its blossom opening
petal by petal as the truth spreads in us:
This is how it is now. Yet the flower finds
calm in the depths, staying immersed
in a process that could take years, until
the eventual unfolding of a self fed by
the darkness it must have cursed at first.

REFLECTIVE PAUSE

Staying Immersed

It is a common phrase among Buddhists—*No mud, no lotus*—and I have heard it said during yoga classes, meditation retreats, and mindfulness circles. Yet the truth of these words applies to people of any faith (or no faith at all), since we all face crises of spirit, hopeless times when we are tempted to give up—or decide to dig deeper. I've weathered many such periods in my own life, when the daily practices of meditation and prayer felt stale and fell away for a while, or when my writing—which I consider another necessary piece of my spiritual practice—seemed like more of a chore than the gift it usually is. What the metaphor of the lotus teaches us is that we, too, can grow and bloom extravagantly out of the mud and muck of confusion, even when feeling underwater. In fact, like the lotus, our souls seem to require the messiness of life in order to grow stronger and help us become just who we are. This does not mean we go about seeking more mud, or even praising it, since none of us would invite more worry and fear into our lives, if we had a choice. Instead, we simply see the clumsy beauty of our struggle as nourishment for the blossoming we all seek. This may take years in the dark to happen, but the time spent in useful rest is never wasted. It will eventually open our heart, petal by petal, to the world exactly as it is, which is the root, for me, of any spiritual practice—to live daily from a place of radical acceptance, saying yes to what's present, and letting it all teach me what I am here to learn.

INVITATION FOR WRITING & REFLECTION:

When in a place of doubt or crisis of faith, what is the most radical, rooted thing you can do for yourself? You might work with this image of the lotus to see what resonates with your own process and practice, writing a set of instructions for yourself about how to stay in a generative darkness that we may want to curse at first.

PART FIVE

The Balm of Attention

Light Show

Before supper, I called upstairs to him:
Come see the light show. And without
a moment's hesitation, he rushed down
to the basement to stand next to me
on the other side of a pool of sun
stretching from the one small window
in the door across the concrete floor.
We watched in silence as light moved
through the leaves of the cherry tree,
mingling with shadows, rippling and
shifting like the mind when you go
quiet enough to isolate each thought—
ever-changing, not made of anything
you can touch. We stood captivated
by that puddle of late light, which
seemed to ask: When was the last time
you dropped everything and danced?

Bright Spot

Coming back from taking out the compost
just after dawn, you pause to look in
your kitchen window where the sun is hitting
the side of a mason jar on the sill,
that bright spot making you stop with
the stained bucket swinging from your hand,
like seeing a scene from someone else's life
for an instant, then realizing that the sink,
dish drain, and arc of faucet are all your own,
that the white light held inside the jar
is yours too, like preserves you can now
spoon onto any plainer moment that might
need a touch of attention to bring it alive.

Komorebi

For what must have been a full minute
in the spacious eternity of an evening
at the ragged end of summer, I stood
in the kitchen as the sun dropped down
behind the trees at the exact right place
for it to dance, shadow and light, across
the swirled grain of the maple counter.
The Japanese call it *komorebi*, this play
of sunshine breaking through the gaps
in leaves, now dappling my hand as I
reach for my mug of tea. One of those
countless small miracles we seldom think
to name in English, a simple reward
for laying down my knife and leaving
a carrot half chopped on the cutting board,
to be here for at least this one out of
the 1,440 minutes I was granted today.

Leap Year

What will you do with this
extra day in the year, these
24 hours dropped at your door
like a gift no one ordered?
Will you stand at the window
speaking to your late mother
through the bare Japanese maple
you planted in her honor—
tangled limbs like a basket
holding starlight just before dawn?
Or will you pray the only way
you know how, by paying attention
to what makes the heart leap—
green blades of the daffodils
slicing through snow, or an eyelash
from your beloved, resting on
the counter like a comma,
begging you to pause right here
before moving on?

World Gratitude Day

I sit on porch steps scoured by last night's rain
next to the holy basil in its terra-cotta pot
with tall, fuzzy stalks sent up from the base
and tiny pink flowers clustered at each tip.

As I sip my tea and try to release the noise
of this world, a bumblebee zooms past
my head, balancing on the filament of a single
blossom to gather pollen from the anther.

I am maybe a foot away, and can hear
the even engine of her flight each time she lands
and takes off again, with no way of knowing
my state has just named her endangered.

I'm so close, I could reach out and touch
the bright-orange pollen sacs on the backs
of her legs, but I don't. I watch, grateful
she's still doing the work she was made for.

Tiger Lily

Like lilies set aflame

I'm unable to hold

anything back.

—Mark Nepo

Sometimes the blaze of a tiger lily
is enough to lift you out of misery.
You go and sit on the mown grass
next to it, offer a sip of your water
as encouragement. Stare long enough,
touch its petals like someone testing
priceless cloth, and you will become
the cup that gathers sun, giving gold
and nectar to whatever winged thing
lands near. Feel yourself sprouting
pistil and stamen, your skin smooth
as velvet now as every reluctant part
of you breaks open for a single day.

Summer Solstice

Peonies bow low to the ground,
petals blown apart and dissolving
back into earth after each rainfall.
Meanwhile, the woodpecker knocks
on the oak door of this summer day,
demanding to be let in. Meanwhile,
the day lily blooms a month early,
orange velvet dusted with a trail
of pollen left by some hurried bee.
And what will we leave behind
when we move on to the nectar
of some other life? I just want to be
remembered as the pond recalls
the shimmer of noon sun, holding
those particles inside its body
as we leap from the dock at dusk.

The Pond at Sunset

I forget I've already arrived
in the life I want, and that I am
still arriving at the same time.
Last night before sunset, I paced
the edge of the dock back and forth,
afraid to take the leap. But as the sun
broke through a rip in the clouds,
strobing across the rippled pond,
the word *Trust* flashed in my mind
and I jumped in. Past the worn-out
desire for a better this or that, past
the fear that if I let my guard down
and just feel joy, something might go
awry, things will fall apart. I cried out
with shock as I rose through colder
layers of water, gasping for air,
spluttering—happier than I've been
in weeks. The pond was my life,
and I knew I had to keep diving
deeper and deeper beneath the surface
to immerse myself in what's already
here, and all that is to come.

REFLECTIVE PAUSE

Diving Deeper

It is a paradox we live out each day—that in order to find the life we want, we have to appreciate and accept the life we already have. No matter how joyful and beautiful, how unpleasant and painful, the heart cries out for full immersion. Yet I have always been an anxious person, which means I am often more comfortable with the familiar and known, like those warmer layers at the top of a pond in summer. I've realized over the years, however, that not diving deeper beneath the surface—not challenging myself enough or trying new things—will keep me in a state of inertia. This all came clear for me recently when my husband and I were swimming in a friend's pond. Once again, I found myself pacing the dock back and forth, even as he tried to coax me into the water, unable to jump in. *You've done this before*, I said to myself, but I couldn't push away the images of what might be waiting under the water—snapping turtles, fish, who knew what else. Then, a sudden light broke through cloud cover, and the word I needed flashed before my eyes—*Trust*. The moment I dove into the water, I knew I was living out a larger metaphor I was being called to embrace.

As Robert Mason has written, "Faith's the courage to risk and receive." If we take the leap, we might meet failure, we might be harmed or disappointed. But if we never risk a thing, we'll never know the rewards, or receive the necessary lessons of those failures. Perhaps as we go through our days, we can all find "timeless moments" like this one, when we feel fully alive to what's here, and awake to what might come.

INVITATION FOR WRITING & REFLECTION:

Describe an instance when you felt caught between risk and reward, between taking a leap or staying safe. When you are able to dive deeper, what allows you to trust the larger container of your life?

August Sunrise

Our minds give off the light
that reveals the connections
linking us one to the other
like the newly risen sun
making visible the dew-
tipped spider webs spun
in the fields last night:
each shining thread drawing
the separate blades of grass
closer together, weaving
a wide patchwork net
which catches everything
that flies into its path.

Craving Quiet

Some days I want to live like a spider
in a quiet corner of the house
where few people step, intricate web
woven where no hands reach, and no one
asks a thing of me. I can't imagine
waiting for food to fall through the roof,
the constant fear of broom and vacuum,
starting over from scratch after each dusting.

But wouldn't it be worth it sometimes?
Not to see another soul for days or weeks,
spinning my own world out of the silk
of stillness—to know the makings of home
are always within me, right here inside the body.

Mother's Day

Then the voice came out of nowhere:
Now, you will have to mother yourself.
The words seemed to ride the wind,
rustling the new leaves on each tree—
its own kind of speech—then disappearing
as soon as those tiny green prayer flags
had settled again. I thought of blue eggs
tucked in the robin's nest I'd found
in a hedge just that morning, perfectly
polished and round, like pieces of sky
the mother had taken into her body
and made into a winged thing kept safe
and warm inside the shell beneath her.
Soft as feathers, the words floated off
to touch someone else who needed them,
needed to be nuzzled back into this
moment, as a doe will nudge her fawn
with her muzzle, as if to say: Stay alert.
I am teaching you how to pay attention
to your life.

Becoming

Don't be afraid to become
something new, something
different, like the windflowers

just now spilling the white
fluff of themselves on every
gust of autumn wind. You have

given enough, and it is time
to move at the pace of a seed
drifting inside this tiny cloud

of possibility, free as a breath
to find a new home in the earth.

That Soft

The mouse nests we cleared
from around the house
were woven with bits
of scavenged pink insulation
and the softest strands
of grass the mice could find.
Finished with our chore
on the last warm day before a storm,
we left the nests in the yard
where they'd soon return to earth.
But I kept thinking, what if
we could take such good care
of each other, make of our days
a safe place to stay.
What if we could be that gentle,
that soft with ourselves.

The Balm of Attention

In what we call the here and now,
wind tosses the tops of bare trees,
bends the pines almost to their knees.
I see this only when the blue of dawn
seeps into the sky, and darkness agrees
to be overtaken by this new light.
So much of our healing stays hidden,
happens in the slim gaps between
one moment and the next. And when
we notice it, feel ourselves pulled
by the winds of attention, what balm
the world spreads on our wounds,
stitching us back together again.

December Sun

With what gratitude we greet you
rising pink above the mountain
before songbirds open their eyes,
or leaving one final orange ember
smoldering behind the tree-line
in the cast-iron woodstove of night.
When nothing else seems promised,
when frozen days turn eerily warm,
and mud swallows every step,
I can at least look up and know
you're still there, returning again
even if I see your longed-for face
just once this morning, like a mother
sending me off into the blustery day
with one last, light kiss on the cheek
still burning even hours later.

Winter Prayer

The world moans this morning,
and the whole house with it.
Snow blows against the windows,
making rippled drifts on each side
of the now impassable driveway.
But I am held here inside this
pool of lamplight with a perfectly
milky cup of steaming coffee
around which I wrap both hands,
my own form of winter prayer.
A blue fleece blanket is draped
over my shoulders, with memories
of every summer I've ever lived
locked inside me—riotous green
leaves bursting my seams, so filled
with heat, all I have to do is
touch the frosted glass, and a small
porthole appears, through which
I can see the light at the end
of this and every storm.

This Fresh Moment

The moment is always fresh,
crisp as the sleet now glazing
the woodpile on the porch.
I feel the sharp points of it,
placing my hand against the ice.
I feel alive, knowing happiness
is harder, though still made of
such small actions: reaching out
to bring a friend closer, squeezing
the arm of her puffy down coat
as we hug. Or sipping water
in which cucumber slices have
steeped for hours, drinking down
the essence of summer, even in
the depths of winter, letting
the glimmer of that clean flavor
guide me like a tiny lantern
out of myself, and into my life.

Winter Joy

What I seek is the deeper joy
of just being here with you,
walking along the icy city street
and tossing a handful of powdery
snow at you, watching the white
spray dissolve in the air. I want
this moment riding every breath
I take in and let out from now on,
muscle memory of our footsteps
and the heart dropping into its own
steady rhythm as I turn to see
your lips stretching into a smile
at the child lying flat on her back
in a sled, pulled by her father,
and a few tears from the cold
frozen at the tips of your lashes,
now catching the light that gathers
around us.

Invincible Summer

Now I understand what it's like
to carry within me an invincible
summer day that can't be touched
by a winter raging and moaning outside.
In this place, perpetual sun caresses
the grass, coaxing mosquitoes up
into the air wherever I step, like
lit embers that hover all around me.
And the black-eyed Susans are always
in bloom, a crowd of yellow in this
quiet, warmer corner of the heart
where monarch caterpillars still
crawl up and down the milkweed,
feasting on leaves and trusting in dreams
that tell of wings tucked somehow
deep inside them.

Joy Is the Only Strategy

Imagine a long corridor
lined with closed doors,
a few bearing your name.
You must choose which one
to step through. Go where
you sense the most joy
waiting on the other side,
a voice drawing you near.
Go where light reaches out
from under the door, where
nothing feels forced, and
the key in your hand just fits.

The Closed Door

Let us bask for a moment
in the beauty of a closed door,
the order imposed by a knob
firmly shut. The world loves
open things—hearts, windows,
a meadow revealed in spring.
But a solid door is its own
form of pleasure, keeping out
unnecessary sounds, voices,
words you don't need. Praise
the hinges that keep working,
swing and click that give you
some breathing room, your body
pressed against the back of it
as your lungs fill and release,
fill and release with ease.

At the Threshold

At the threshold of freedom and change,
even the monarch will still cling
to the empty sleeve of the chrysalis
as if it held some clue—and perhaps
it does, proving that we cannot let go
of what birthed us so easily, cannot
abandon the dark place that became
our home right away, even when
it no longer serves us. Maybe it's awe
that keeps the butterfly holding on,
asking: How did I come from *this*?
Eyes adjusting to relentless summer light,
sensing the need for answers will soon
vanish with that first stuttering flight.

At the River

He pointed to the place on the shaded stone
where light-blue and gray butterflies
known as spring azures had gathered
to drink and cool off for a moment,
but when he stepped closer in flip-flops,
they all lifted off at once and fluttered
around him as he put out his arms
and looked down, smiling at the flock
he seemed to be guiding with strings
tied to his fingers, while I marveled
at the man standing before me—the luck
of our meeting—and my own heart beating
its frantic wings in sweet confusion
and wonder on that endless summer day.

The Sense of Wonder

What if wonder is the other sense
you've been missing all your life
in the blinding cloud of busyness,
and you access it again just by
sitting in a patch of sun on the couch,
skin warmed by rare November light
as you talk to a friend on the phone,
that familiar voice its own kind
of brightness, every shared word
a drop of honey on the tongue
you'll go on tasting for days.

Beyond Burnout

I knew I had to say no to busyness
when the thought of my canceled flights
and postponed meetings made me feel
like a red-tailed hawk with wings
stretched wide, soft white undersides
visible only from a field far below.
I knew I had to change my life when
I began to dream of an empty room
with houseplants stuck in their pots,
all of them neglected, shriveled, in need
of water and care. Each time I said yes
to myself, I became a patch of ground
where anything might grow, forgotten
seeds and once-crowded roots now
with room to spread and reach, now
with space to seek what they need.

REFLECTIVE PAUSE

Saying Yes to Yourself

Whether burned out by work, caregiving, or grief, we all know the telltale fatigue that falls over us, and that sense of just pushing ahead. We may keep things going, though without the ability to take joy in what we're doing. It can be humbling when we finally recognize the burnout we stumbled into yet again, having become what Jon Kabat-Zinn calls a "human-doing," instead of a human being. In the middle of my own exhaustion, when someone finally gave me permission to think beyond the pull of all my responsibilities, I felt a soaring inside, as if I was the red-tailed hawk I'd noticed on one of my walks—circling overhead, soft and strong, steady and free at the same time. I also began to dream of an apartment that I was still renting but had somehow forgotten about, all the houseplants shriveled, left untended and unwatered in their pots. After several nights of this same dream, I started to see the wisdom of saying yes to myself, even if it felt like an unnecessary indulgence. This is how we begin to meet our needs, naming them for ourselves, speaking them out loud or writing them down, being willing to disappoint the people around us who may or may not understand our need for solitude, space, and time for play (or whatever brings us alive again). It may feel unfamiliar and wrong at first, but we might be surprised by what grows in the bare patch of ground we become, a subtle wildness taking over as we let ourselves do less, and in the process become so much more.

INVITATION FOR WRITING & REFLECTION:

Have there been times in your life when you've had to say no to busyness in order to look after your health and well-being? What did it feel like when you finally recognized your own burnout? To write, you might begin with, "I knew I had to change my life when . . ." and see what feels most true to you.

About the Author

JAMES CREWS is the editor of several bestselling books, including *The Path to Kindness* and *How to Love the World*, which has more than a hundred thousand copies in print. He has been featured in *The Washington Post*, *The Boston Globe*, *The New York Times Magazine*, *The New Republic*, *The Christian Science Monitor*, and on NPR's *Morning Edition*. The author of numerous prize-winning books of poetry, including *Unlocking the Heart*, and of the book *Kindness Will Save the World*, James also speaks and leads workshops on kindness, mindfulness, and writing for self-compassion. He lives with his husband on forty rocky acres in the woods of Southern Vermont. For more info, and to sign up for free weekly poems and writing prompts, visit: JamesCrews.net

MANDALA

An Imprint of MandalaEarth
PO Box 3088
San Rafael, CA 94912
www.MandalaEarth.com

Publisher Raoul Goff
Associate Publisher Roger Shaw
Assistant Editor Amanda Nelson
Managing Editor Michelle Hope
Creative Director Ashley Quackenbush
Senior Designer Stephanie Odeh
VP Manufacturing Alix Nicholaeff
Senior Production Manager Joshua Smith
Strategic Production Planner Lina s Palma-Temena

MandalaEarth would also like to thank Ellen Foreman.

ISBN: 979-8-88762-151-7

Manufactured in China by Insight Editions

10 9 8 7 6 5 4 3 2 1

ROOTS of PEACE REPLANTED PAPER

Insight Editions, in association with Roots of Peace, will plant two trees for each tree used in the manufacturing of this book. Roots of Peace is an internationally renowned humanitarian organization dedicated to eradicating land mines worldwide and converting war-torn lands into productive farms and wildlife habitats. Roots of Peace will plant two million fruit and nut trees in Afghanistan and provide farmers there with the skills and support necessary for sustainable land use.